I0030767

PUBLISHED BY
ScientificSelection Press
36 Emerson Hill Square
Marietta, Georgia 30060

ISBN 0-9711904-0-2

For more information contact Scientific Selection. Telephone 770-792-6857, or visit our web site at ScientificSelection.com.

The example companies, organizations, products, people, and events depicted herein are fictitious and are in no way intended to represent any real individual, company, product, or event unless otherwise noted.

Cover/Layout: Iconix.biz

About the Author

R. Wendell Williams, PhD

Wendell is Managing Director of ScientificSelection.com, llc. He is a nationally recognized expert at measuring job skills. His academic training and broad career experience enables him to apply hard research about human motivation and job performance to real world challenges. He has built competency-based organizational systems, used pattern-recognition software to identify and select high performance workers, and identified personality factors that affect job performance. Additionally, Wendell has consulted with senior executives and managers in both national and international organizations, built computerized assessment systems, and developed customized tests and surveys.

His tools include job analysis, test validation, test development, behavioral interview technology, and realistic simulations. Over the years, Wendell has built systems that enable organizations to measure and enhance employee performance. He has served a wide variety of Fortune 1000 clients, many of which are industry leaders. Wendell holds a BS, MBA, MS, and a PhD in industrial psychology. Before establishing ScientificSelection.com, Wendell served as senior consultant & team leader in the Atlanta office of Development Dimensions International (DDI), an international organization that specializes in assessment, training and development. He is a member of the American Psychological Association and The Society for Industrial/Organizational Psychologists.

You can find out more about the services Wendell offers by visiting ScientificSelection.com.

Contents

LESSON IV: PREPARING FOR THE INTERVIEW   21

LESSON V: MEASURING APPLICANT COMPETENCIES   28

LESSON VI: ERRORS AND OMISSIONS   33

LESSON VII: OTHER BEHAVIORAL INTERVIEWING APPLICATIONS

FINAL EXAM   42

APPENDIX A: SUMMARY   47

APPENDIX B: COMPETENCY WORKSHEETS   48

APPENDIX C: SAMPLE QUESTION WORKSHEET   68

SuperSelection

R. Wendell Williams, PhD

LESSON I

Selection and Placement Basics

INTERVIEWS ARE TESTS

Before we begin, it is important to realize that any system used to compare an applicant to job requirements is a test. That is, you test job applicants to see if they have the right skills for the job. Job applications, interviews, traditional tests, performance reviews, and promotion criteria are all different forms of tests. Just as professors test students to find out how much knowledge they have absorbed in a course, interviewers "test" applicants to find out what job skills they bring to a job.

As you progress through this course, keep in mind, that like a good test, a good interview has three major characteristics:

1) Interview content is directly related to the job

2) Interviewees are all exposed to the same testing conditions

3) There is one standard answer key

Let's see how these characteristics work during an interview. Because human behavior tends to repeat itself, historical job-related behavior can be a valuable source of information. If the interviewer is able to gather accurate examples of the applicant's past performance, then reasonably accurate predictions can be made about the future. However, because jobs are often very different, an effective interviewer must also be able to "translate" data from the old job to the new job.

Translation requires using a consistent system of open-ended, behavioral-based questions. This exposes each applicant to the same test conditions. After interviewers finish gathering accurate data about the applicant's skills, they convert the information into competencies and compare responses with job requirements. This format "standardizes" interview answers.

TRADITIONAL INTERVIEWS

Most traditional interviews fail to meet any of the requirements of a good test.

How often have you seen an interviewer not know what to ask the applicant, use different questions with different applicants, talk about everything but job skills, allow personality factors to affect judgment, ask foolish questions, be swayed by personal appearance, or overlook important data?

What if a professor gave you a test in which the content had little to do with what you learned over the semester, there was no answer key against which to check your responses, and each student took an entirely different test. In such conditions, how could the professor judge which of the students learned the material?

That's why traditional interviews only have a fifty/fifty chance of predicting whether or not an applicant can do the job and an almost zero percent chance of predicting the actual level of job performance. In other words, *traditional interviewing is no better than flipping a coin: you only have a 50% chance of being right.* This type of corporate gamble results in huge turnover, excessive training expenses, a significant loss of individual productivity, and the nasty possibility of getting sued for unfair hiring practices.

BEHAVIORAL INTERVIEWS

The behavioral interviewing process is very different. It still gives the interviewer a chance to get to know the applicant, but it uses three very special techniques to improve accuracy:

> **1)** A job analysis to define, validate and establish performance criteria,
>
> **2)** A consistent set of open-ended questions and special questioning techniques that gather accurate information,
>
> **3)** A way to "score" applicant answers.

When you master behavioral interviewing, you will:

> ♦ Help your organization look more professional to applicants,
>
> ♦ Gather better, more accurate information,
>
> ♦ Reduce hiring risk,
>
> ♦ Add legal credibility to your selection process (if you are subject to US laws).

But, above all, personal productivity will soar!

UP CLOSE AND PERSONAL WITH THE FEDS

I know, you want to get right to the interview questions. But, like it or not, you should know your profession is subject to some very important laws. Non-US interviewers don't need to worry about American employment laws. But the folks who wrote US law followed the advice of experts whose methods work just as well beyond American borders as within them. In short, whether you do business in the US or not, these behavioral interviewing practices will work for you!

For those of you not subject to US law, just focus on the effectiveness part. For those affected by US law, be sure to think about both effectiveness and legal requirements. Don't consider this program as legal advice -- that's what labor attorneys are for -- just use it to master a few placement and selection basics.

EMPLOYMENT LAW

Employment practices are covered by the Civil Rights Act of 1964 (CRA). Since its inception, the CRA has been steadily expanded and amended by Congress and by Executive Order. We won't worry about the entire CRA here, only the section that currently affects selection of job applicants. Part 60-3 of the **UNIFORM GUIDELINES ON EMPLOYEE SELECTION PROCEDURES (1978)** is very long and detailed, but here are a few of the major provisions you ought to know:

> ♦ It is illegal to discriminate against people on the basis of age, gender, or race for hiring, promotion, or other employment or membership opportunities.
>
> ♦ A selection rate for any race, sex, or ethnic group which is less than 80% (4/5) of the selection rate for the majority group with the highest selection rate will generally be regarded as evidence of discrimination (more on this later).
>
> ♦ A job analysis is necessary to show that a selection system is fair and equitable.
>
> ♦ Any method used for selection must be validated (i.e., proven to be directly related to the job).
>
> ♦ You are not required to hire anyone who is unqualified, but you must document that your selection tools are fair, equitable, based on business need, and real job requirements.

PLACEMENT REGULATIONS

The "Guidelines" incorporate a single set of principles which are designed to assist employers, labor organizations, employment agencies, and licensing and certification boards to comply with requirements of federal law prohibiting employment practices which discriminate on basis of race, color, religion, sex, and national origin. They are designed to provide a framework for determining the proper use of tests and other selection procedures. They have been adopted by the Equal Employment Opportunity Commission, the Department of Labor, the Department of Justice, and the Civil Service Commission.

The law is continually being reinterpreted by the courts, so you should always discuss selection issues with an experienced labor law attorney. The full DOL document can be viewed on the Department of Labor website at **www.dol.gov/dol/allcfr/Title_41/Part_60-3/toc.htm**.

By the way, the definition of a "selection procedure" as used here is very broad. Basically, it is ANY measure, combination of measures or procedure used to make an employment decision. This includes methods such as traditional paper and pencil tests, performance tests, training programs, probationary periods, physical requirements, educational requirements, work experience, informal or casual interviews, scored and unscored application forms, etc.

"UNFAIR" AND "FAIR" DISCRIMINATION (US LAWS)

Unless they hire everyone who applies, organizations practice discrimination all the time. They discriminate between the qualified and the unqualified. It is a perfectly legal practice. The government only gets involved when employers start straying away from actual job requirements. The government's objective is the same as yours: to ignore unimportant things like race, age, or gender and concentrate exclusively on whether or not applicants are qualified for the job.

The Feds have a specific test, called The 80% Rule, that serves as a benchmark for what is called "adverse impact." We'll use a simple example to illustrate how the test works. Suppose you interviewed 120 people for a job. Ninety-five were white males and twenty-five were minority males. Now, suppose you hired 60 of the white males. According to the 80% rule, if you did not hire 13 minority males, you engaged in illegal discrimination.

Confused? Let's do some math.

1) The number of white males interviewed = 95

2) Now, the number of white males who were hired and the percentage of hired vs. interviewed: white males hired (60) divided by white males interviewed (95) = 63%

3) Take 80% times the hiring rate calculated above: 80% x 63% = 51%

4) Next, multiply the test percentage by number of minorities interviewed: 51% x Minority interviewed (25) = 13 minority hires required. If you did not hire 13 of the 25 minorities who applied, the EEOC will consider your selection system discriminatory.

The question the Feds would want answered is, "Can you show us documented evidence that your selection system is based on business necessity and job requirements?"

What will your answer be?

JOB ANALYSIS: THE BEGINNING AND THE ENDING

Companies create jobs not as a public service but because they have problems to solve. The company must hire someone with specific talents or skills to fill a specific need. Employees may be given some say over how they do their jobs, but they still must accomplish the basic task they were hired to do. Applicants should be hired based on how well they can perform those basic tasks.

Basic tasks and the behaviors used to achieve them are uncovered using a technique called "job analysis." A job analysis is a professionally conducted study of what it takes to do a job. Although there may be slight overlap, a job analysis is not a job description and it is not a job salary evaluation. Let's explain.

A job description primarily defines why a job exists, its scope of responsibility, reporting relationships, and general outcomes. It is usually written in broad terms and does not discuss how a job is to be done. Job evaluations are used to determine what a job is worth, or how much someone in that position should be paid.

Evaluations include many factors that have nothing to do with job performance such as supply/demand for applicants, market factors, job tenure, and geographic cost of living. When you try to combine job analysis with job salary evaluation and job descriptions, you will soon find yourself in a whole heap of trouble.

IMPORTANCE OF COMPETENCIES

Unlike job evaluations and job descriptions, job analysis defines "how" a job is to be performed. In the academic world these are called "dimensions of performance". In the business world, they are often referred to as "job competencies." Competencies are the skills, knowledge, and attitudes that any person who fills the job must have to be successful. When employees' personal competencies match job competencies, the job gets done well. When employees do not have the right competencies for the job, performance suffers.

A good behavioral interviewer never ventures into an interview without knowing the exact competencies required for the job.

Critical competencies are determined by interviewing experts in your company about the job. This includes asking jobholders what they do, managers what they expect from jobholders and senior managers about how the job might change in the future. This gives you a detailed list of job tasks based on three perspectives.

Unfortunately, a long list of detailed tasks is not very helpful in selection, so you must convert the specific job tasks into "competencies." Using competencies allows you to gather task information from a past job and use this information to predict performance in a future job.

You will learn more about competencies later in this course.

THE CONCEPT OF "VALIDITY"

After you determine the competencies required for the job, you must choose accurate tools to measure them. These tools include tests, cases, biographical data, weighted application blanks, simulations, role-plays, exercises, and of course, interviews.

Regardless of which testing method you use, you need to determine whether the test scores are related to job performance. This is called "validation." Essentially, you want to prove that your test results can be trusted.

There are three methods for validating a test:

- ♦ **Content validation:** Does the content of the test resemble the content of the job?
- ♦ **Criterion validation:** Do higher test scores predict higher job performance?
- ♦ **Construct validation:** Does the test measure deep-seated mental constructs that are associated with job performance?

The different validation types can be explained using the example of a job analysis for a data entry clerk. Suppose the job analysis identified typing letters as a critical part of job success.

- ♦ Content Validity: A test that required an applicant to type a letter would be "content valid," meaning that passing the test would indicate whether or not the applicant could type.
- ♦ Criterion Related Validity: If higher scores on the typing test were associated with better performance on the job, the test would meet the requirements for "criterion-related" validity.
- ♦ Construct Validity: Finally, if you discovered that "attitude" had something to do with keyboard skills, you could give each applicant an attitude test. However, you would have the burden of proving that attitude (a construct) predicted typing ability. Construct validity is often very hard to identify or interpret - and the Feds advise against using it!

TRANSPOSING JOB VALIDATION DATA

A common error among many clients is to rely on validity data from another organization. For example, if Aaco Steel conducts a validation study for a machinist test, Beeco Steel, wanting to save the costs of performing their own study, might attempt to use the same test and scores to select its machinists. You should **avoid this practice** unless you have done a job analysis that shows the machinist jobs at both companies are essentially the same.

INTERVIEW VALIDITY

Traditional interviews do not meet any of the criteria for validation. As we mentioned earlier, they work poorly, if at all. Some of the major reasons for poor interview validity include not knowing what to ask, using different questions for each applicant, using questions that have nothing to do with the job, having personal biases, having unclear job requirements, not exploring every competency required for the job, and not having a good way to evaluate answers.

A behavioral interviewing system on the other hand is a valid technique for selecting between job applicants because:

- ♦ Competency requirements are clearly defined
- ♦ Questions directly relate to job requirements
- ♦ Behavioral interview techniques reduce error
- ♦ The various aspects of the job are thoroughly covered by the interview
- ♦ Questions probe past on-the-job behavior
- ♦ Information from the interview is measured using a standard "answer key"

Consider for example, a telephone sales position:

- ♦ **Persuasiveness Competency:** the ability to persuade people to follow a course of action they would not normally take.
- ♦ **Sample Interview Question and Behavioral Interview Technique:** Give me an example of a time when you had to sell a difficult prospect. What was the situation? What did you do? What was the result?
- ♦ Other competencies and questions might probe Tenacity, Planning, Motivational Fit, Written Communication Skills, Problem Solving, etc.
- ♦ A standard answer key for Persuasiveness questions might include listening to the prospect, clarifying the need, empathizing with the prospects feelings, clarifying the issues, presenting benefits, converting objections to questions, and asking for the sale.

SUMMARY

It is important to realize that interviews are considered to be tests just as much as their pencil and paper "cousins." In fact, interview effectiveness depends on following the same guidelines, such as content validity, controlled administration and standardized answer keys. Traditional interviews are highly inaccurate and error-filled because they do not follow good test standards. Behavioral interviewing can be at least ten to twenty-five times more accurate than traditional interviews because it uses a system of job analysis, behavioral interviewing techniques and a uniform scoring system. US law recommends that employers use the kind of system employed by behavioral interviewing. The EEOC tests organizations for Adverse Impact using the 80% rule. Job analysis is a systematic way to determine the business need and required job competencies used in selection systems. Every method used to select applicants needs to be professionally validated to demonstrate its effectiveness as a selection tool. It is perfectly legal to discriminate against anyone who does not meet clearly defined job criteria based on business need and business necessity.

TEST YOUR HIRING KNOW HOW

1) Put these in chronological order:

   a) Developing an "answer key"

   b) Doing an 80% test

   c) Developing job competencies

   d) Conducting a behavioral interview

2) 350 applicants apply for a job. 300 are members of non-protected groups and the rest are members of protected groups. 200 people from the non-protected group are offered a job. If some nasty attorney were to "test" your selection system for Adverse Impact, how would he determine the critical number?

   a) Divide 300 by 350 and multiply by 80%

   b) Divide 300 by 200 and multiply the result by 80%

   c) Divide 200 by 300, multiply the result by 80%, then multiply by 50

   d) Divide 50 by 80% then multiply by 300 and subtract 350

3) Data gathered from traditional interviews is:

   a) Highly unreliable

   b) More of a conversation than a test

   c) Widespread

   d) All of the above

4) True or False: All a good interviewer needs is a list of tried and true questions.

5) Mark each characteristic with a "B" for behavioral interviewing, or a "T" for traditional interviewing.

   a) 50/50 effectiveness

   b) Competency based

   c) Content valid

   d) Error-filled

   e) Legally credible

   f) More professional

   g) Most common

   h) Does not meet validity standards

   i) Reduces turnover

   j) Systematic

   k) Takes more skill to use

   l) Tends to have adverse impact

   m) Usually based on job description

6) Match the items on the left with the items on the right.

1. A test of programming ability   a) Content validity

2. A test of programming skills   b) Construct validity

3. A test of programming performance   c) Criterion validity

LESSON II

Fundamentals of a Job Analysis

COMPETENCY CLUSTERS

Behavioral interviewing works because it is part of a system - one that includes identifying and measuring critical competencies, as well as evaluating responses from applicants. But everything starts with understanding what it takes to do a job.

Regardless of the job or position, all job competencies fall into a few general areas:

♦ **Problem Solving:** The ability to learn, analyze problems and make decisions.

♦ **Planning:** The ability to plan and organize work.

♦ **Interpersonal:** The ability to get things done through others; could include coaching, basic teamwork, persuasion, customer service, presentation skills, etc.

♦ **Attitudes, Interests and Motivations:** An assortment of Attitudes, Interests and Motivations that affects everything else.

♦ **Physical requirements:** (not relevant for some job types)

For example, a structural engineer must be able to solve problems, communicate ideas to team members, and enjoy doing the job. A sales person might be required to analyze customer problems, persuade prospects to purchase products, and enjoy working on commission. Of course, jobs are much more complex than these simple examples.

JOB COMPETENCIES

Think of a competency in a job-centric way. That is, a competency is a special skill needed by anyone who is expected to perform the job. Competencies are based on what the job is expected to produce, not on who does the job. Before you can go applicant hunting, you have to develop a competency list.

In general, the simpler the job, the fewer the competencies. A cleaning crew job might have 3 to 4 competencies, while a professional or mid-manager job might require 12 to 14 of them. Very senior executive jobs have unique competencies that are exceedingly hard to identify and measure. Only a very competent and experienced job analyst should ever tackle a senior management position.

Use only as many competencies as you can measure. As you increase the number of competencies, there will be more and more overlap between them. For example, the competency "analysis" could be subdivided into "marketing" analysis, "financial" analysis, "stress" analysis, or "operational" analysis. Regardless of what you call it, analysis still involves digging for information and figuring out what to do. Only the technical knowledge changes.

Understanding competencies is the first step in behavioral interviewing.

COMPETENCY TYPES AND MEASUREMENT

People obviously do not normally think or talk in terms of competencies. Some people can't even spell "competency," let alone develop a competency list. There are a variety of definitions that people use when talking about "competency," but only one of them can help us in behavioral interviewing.

♦ Definition 1: "Our organizational competency is making teeny-tiny machines." Forget that one.

♦ Definition 2: "Competencies help people manage and understand the job." Nope.

♦ Definition 3: "Competencies are used to determine training needs." Uh-uh.

♦ Definition 4: "Competencies are special skills needed by a successful job applicant when filling the job." Finally! This is the one we can work with!

Competencies used for behavioral interviewing are fairly straightforward. They are used (in varying amounts) across many positions; they do not change with time; they describe differences in performance; and most of all, **THEY ARE MEASURABLE!**

MEASURABILITY

Making sure that competencies are measurable is subtle but critical. Being a "hard worker" or being "dedicated" might sound good, but how in the world do you measure that kind of thing without asking the obvious question, "Are you a hard worker?" You will most certainly get the obvious answer.

You must discover what being a "hard worker" looks like on the job. Did the applicant take the initiative and start programs that saved the company money or led to greater efficiency? Did they follow up on tasks assigned? Did they seek out new projects when current projects ended? What did they do or say to qualify as a hard worker?

Your job is to discover the actual, measurable behaviors it takes to accomplish the job. If you don't have a list of measurable behaviors, you will end up with a lot of opinions and flimflam that will sound impressive, but will be useless when you try to measure anybody against anything.

MEASURING APPLICANT BEHAVIOR

The only thing you can actually measure in an interview is behavior (i.e., the "what did you do?" part of the behavioral interview). An applicant who says "I worked hard" hasn't told you a thing about what was actually done. Think of applicant behaviors as the bricks that make up one wall of a house. You need to build a brick wall of information based on the behaviors elicited during the interview. If you lack information because you did not ask the right questions, or if the applicant did not demonstrate the proper behaviors to indicate a good worker, then you will end up with a very weak wall.

Thinking of a position in measurable behaviors will help you organize and systematically cover all the information you need to collect from the applicant. Since applicants usually come from different jobs and backgrounds, comparing competency-related behaviors in a past job will help considerably to bridge the gap to competencies needed for the job at hand.

NON-MEASURABLE ITEMS

Here is a list of common terms or phrases you will hear people use to describe what they do on the job. You will need to translate them into behaviors before you can measure them:

- ♦ Hard worker
- ♦ Conscientious
- ♦ Team player
- ♦ Positive attitude
- ♦ Gets along with others
- ♦ Stick to it
- ♦ Good "fit"
- ♦ Cares about quality
- ♦ A "people person"
- ♦ Good communicator
- ♦ Likes the work
- ♦ Supports the organization
- ♦ Sees the "big picture"

None of these phrases is particularly helpful, since just about any applicant can claim them (although not necessarily with justification.) You need to put meaning into these phrases by probing for "hard" descriptions of behaviors that demonstrate these empty phrases. Take, for example, the phrase "Team Player." A better description would be *"Actively supports team members by offering to help."*

DISCOVERING CRITICAL, MEASURABLE JOB COMPETENCIES

The job analysis is where you get information to start the behavioral interview process. It is also, coincidentally, where you will finish. A job analysis is generally conducted by a member of the human resources staff in a large company, or the person in charge of hiring in a smaller company. But regardless of who performs the analysis, it should contain the same basic information and follow the same process. Job analysis involves gathering information from three separate groups of people who are considered to be job experts. Specifically:

- ♦ Four to five typical jobholders who have been in the job long enough to know it. (Avoid both the highest and lowest performers. You will get the best data from average to above-average performers who have been on the job from 9 to 12 months.)
- ♦ Two or three managers of jobholders.
- ♦ A senior manager.

In the following pages you will see how to conduct a basic job analysis. There are many other formats and job analysis methods to use, but this one will get you what you need for a behavioral interview.

CHOOSING JOB EXPERTS

Not all job analyses will include this many people. You might be able to find four to five data clerks to interview who perform substantially the same job, but finding four to five senior vice presidents who perform exactly the same job might be a bit more difficult. Also, be sure to include as many members of protected or under-represented groups in your analysis as you can.

You will notice that we have not considered human resources personnel to be job content experts. This is because HR staff members are often removed from the job and seldom know as much about job performance as the jobholder, manager or senior line manger. HR people can learn a great deal more about a job than they ever imagined when they facilitate a job analysis.

MEETING PREPARATION

You want to appear well informed when you talk to job content experts, so learn something about the job before you begin asking questions. Study job advertisements, job descriptions, training programs or anything else that can prepare you for interviews with job content experts. This will help make your questions as pertinent as possible.

Jobholders usually know a great deal more than anyone else about the details of the work. They will often tell you things no one else knows. Since it usually takes some time to understand what a job requires, you should choose people who have worked in the job for at least nine months.

Don't choose the highest job performers for your job analysis, or employees who have been on the job since the invention of the steam engine. It sounds strange, but a high performer is not the typical worker; high performers often take shortcuts. You want people who know the job and can describe it thoroughly. Average and above-average workers provide the most comprehensive data.

You also need to think about your experts' age, gender and racial background. Get a good mix of people. Even though they all do the same job, demographically diverse job experts will show that you went out of your way to minimize age, gender, or racial bias.

Remember: when you interview people you must assure them that your purpose is to learn about what's needed for the job, not about their personal performance.

SUMMARY

Competencies are the ultimate goal of doing a job analysis. Competencies are associated with job performance regardless of who fills the position. All competencies fall into one of four general areas. Simple jobs have fewer competencies (three to four,) and complex jobs have more. Most jobs will have 12-14 competencies. The most important part of a competency is that it can be measured. People use many terms to "define" what they do on the job. It is the job analyst's responsibility to convert meaningless terms such as "hard worker" and "team player" into measurable behaviors that are associated with competencies.

People who participate in a job analysis are called "job content experts." They are usually people who do the job, manage the job and/or decide how the job will change in the future. Choosing job experts consists of selecting people with diverse backgrounds of race, gender and age, and who have enough experience to provide useful information.

TEST YOUR HIRING KNOW HOW

1) Label each competency with it's proper competency area: Problem Solving, Planning, Interactive Skills, Attitudes, Interests and Motivations, or None.

> a) Learning
>
> b) Age
>
> c) Team work
>
> d) Planning
>
> e) Time management
>
> f) Persuasion
>
> g) Technical knowledge
>
> h) Interests
>
> i) Coaching
>
> j) Judgment
>
> k) Racial background
>
> l) Attitudes
>
> m) Analysis
>
> n) Motivations
>
> o) Gender
>
> p) Customer service skill
>
> q) Importance of work

2) True or false: Job competencies depend on who is filling the job.

3) A job analyst left abruptly on vacation. You picked up his notes and read the following information. Place a mark beside each behavior that you could easily measure using an interview.

> a) works hard
>
> b) asks people questions to clarify what they mean
>
> c) supports the organization by volunteering for projects
>
> d) is a team player
>
> e) actively solves problems
>
> f) is a leader
>
> g) makes suggestions to improve processes
>
> h) has a good attitude
>
> i) is a good fit for the job

4) Who should be included in a job analysis as a job expert?

  a) people who have 8 months with the organization, and 5 years job experience

  b) males under 40 with 2-3 years job experience

  c) the very best performers

  d) performers with the longest job tenure

  e) managers from other departments

  f) average and above average performers

  g) a sampling of age, race and gender regardless of performance

  h) customers

  i) managers of job holders

  j) human resource staff

LESSON III

Conducting the Job Analysis

GATHERING DEMOGRAPHIC DATA

Before you start a meeting with a job expert as part of your job analysis, be sure to record the following demographic information. It is unlikely that you will ever need the information, but it serves as a record in case of future complaints or investigations. The information will help show the diversity of your job experts and the breadth of their knowledge.

- ♦ Name of the expert
- ♦ Position
- ♦ Age (over/under 40)
- ♦ Gender
- ♦ Race (Caucasian, African American, Hispanic, Asian American, Pacific Islander, Native American, Other)
- ♦ Amount of job experience
- ♦ Experience with the organization

Remember: this data should be kept somewhere safe. It will serve as legal documentation in case you should ever need it.

GATHERING INFORMATION FROM JOBHOLDERS

The first type of job expert you will interview is the person who actually holds the job. You can meet with jobholders in a group or one-on-one. It is okay to give them your list of questions before the meeting. Use the following open-ended questions to gather information. Be careful not to "lead" the answers. You should tailor this list to the individual position, but here are some general suggestions:

- ♦ What kind of decisions do the jobholders have to make?
- ♦ What kind of special technical knowledge is required to start the job?
- ♦ What important things need to be learned and applied?
- ♦ What kind of planning skills are needed?
- ♦ What kinds of team member interactions occur frequently?
- ♦ What kind of customer contact occurs frequently?
- ♦ What kind of persuasion is required?
- ♦ How important is quality to the job?
- ♦ What makes the job enjoyable?
- ♦ What makes the job unpleasant?
- ♦ What challenges does a new employee face on the job?
- ♦ What kind of presentations are required?
- ♦ What kind of reports need to be written?

Here is a sample script:

"Thank you for coming to this meeting. I'm trying to learn more about your job by asking some questions. Although the questions will be directed at you, all I really want to know is what the job requires. I'm not interested in how the job 'should be done' just how it is being done now. I'll be writing everything down, and combining all the answers that I hear into one big list. Your individual answers will be completely anonymous. Ready?"

GATHERING INFORMATION FROM MANAGERS

Managers often do not know the details of the job, but they do know about overall performance. When you talk to managers, tell them you do not want names, but you need to gather information about jobholder performance. Some of the questions you might ask include:

- ♦ Why are people hired or fired from the position?
- ♦ What examples can you give that illustrate above-average performance?
- ♦ What examples can you give that illustrate below-average performance?

These three questions are usually enough to generate a substantial conversation. As with the jobholder interviews, write everything down and check for measurable behaviors.

Here is your sample script:

> "Thank you for coming to this meeting. I'm trying to learn more about the "XYZ" job by asking some questions. You are in a position to comment on both good and bad performance. I'm not interested in how the job should be done just how it is being done now. I'll be writing everything down, and combining all the answers that I hear into one big list. Your individual answers will be completely anonymous. Ready?"

GATHERING INFORMATION FROM SENIOR MANAGERS

Senior managers seldom give you specific details about the responsibility of the position for which you will be hiring. However, they usually know more about future job changes than anyone else.

Before you meet with the senior manager, consolidate your job analysis data into one document. Give the document to the manager to study, and ask whether the job requirements will be changing in the immediate future.

You should ask the manager the following questions:

- ♦ Do you see anything on this list that will change within the next two years?
- ♦ Is there anything I should add?
- ♦ Is there anything I should delete?
- ♦ Is there anything I should change?

Carefully write down the manager's responses.

Here is your sample script:

> "Thank you for taking time to meet with me. I'm trying to learn more about the "XYZ" job by asking some questions. You are in a position to comment on how you see the job changing in the future. I'll be taking notes and combining all the answers that I hear into one big list for us to use in selection. Here is a list of what I have learned so far. Do you have any questions?"

ORGANIZING YOUR DATA

By now you should have:

- ♦ The demographics of each person in your job analysis
- ♦ Hands-on information from each job holder
- ♦ Performance opinions from each manager
- ♦ Some idea of whether the job will change over the next two years
- ♦ Pages full of specific job behaviors and competencies

Unfortunately, pages of details are not very useful interviewing tools. These behaviors must now be translated into **Action Statements** and then assigned to **Competencies.**

TRANSLATING NOTES INTO ACTION STATEMENTS

Translating job behaviors into Action Statements puts your data into context, makes it easier to classify as a competency and helps you evaluate applicant answers. For example, you might have learned that it was the responsibility of the jobholder to work on a marketing team to come up with ideas about how to market the new model of plungers the company sells.

Translating this responsibility into an Action Statement is fairly straightforward. Simply distill the requirement into *a behavior and an outcome*. The resulting Action Statement might be: "Brainstorm with colleagues to create plunger marketing ideas."

Behavior = to brainstorm with colleagues

Outcome = marketing ideas about plungers.

Be careful not to put too much or too little information in an Action Statement. Keep it simple.

Poor Action Statement Examples:

"Questions customers" (not enough data)

"Questions customers to determine needs so that solutions can be presented" (too much data)

Good Action Statement Example:

"Questions customers to discover potential problems"

Go through your notes and convert them into Action Statements. Eliminate duplicates, simplify complex statements and try to combine similar behaviors into single statements.

COMMON JOB COMPETENCIES

Your job expert questions help you formulate key job activities called "Action Statements." As we mentioned before, if you look closely at the data you collected, you will see that all your items can be combined into four to five main skill clusters. Examining the information collected in each of these clusters will help you:

- ◆ Cover the job thoroughly and completely,
- ◆ Avoid concentrating too heavily on one part of the job at the expense of the others,
- ◆ Make better, more accurate, placement decisions.

The Skill Clusters include:

- ◆ Problem Solving
- ◆ Planning
- ◆ Interpersonal
- ◆ Attitudes, Interests and Motivations
- ◆ Physical (most important for jobs that have significant physical components)

PROBLEM SOLVING CLUSTER

Now you are ready to classify your Action Statements into competency areas. Remember, a competency must be measurable to be useful.

Problem Solving competencies vary greatly between jobs. Both a janitor and an executive management position require some degree of problem solving, but a management position requires more depth of knowledge and wider scope.

Action Statements within the Problem Solving Cluster should address the need for learning and applying information to solve problems. Within each competency be sure to include how much (scope) and how detailed (depth) the job requires of the person to be effective.

Problem Solving competencies typically include:

- ◆ Possessing a certain type of technical knowledge
- ◆ Knowing how to use technical tools, etc.
- ◆ Ability to thoroughly analyze job-related problems
- ◆ Ability to make well-considered decisions
- ◆ Ability to learn and apply new information
- ◆ Making good, on-time decisions
- ◆ Developing strategies to accomplish a goal

PLANNING CLUSTER

Planning competencies vary between jobs just as much as Problem Solving competencies. Using our earlier example, both a janitor and an executive management position require some degree of planning, but a management position requires more depth and wider scope. Remember, a competency must be measurable to be useful.

Your Action Statements within the Planning Cluster should address the need for sequencing activities and keeping track of tasks. Within each competency be sure to include how much (scope) and how detailed (depth) the job requires of the person to be effective.

Planning competencies typically include:

- ◆ Tracking tasks and activities
- ◆ Monitoring processes or tasks
- ◆ Planning projects
- ◆ Time management
- ◆ Territory management
- ◆ Planning for contingencies
- ◆ Following up on assignments

INTERPERSONAL CLUSTER

Interpersonal competencies do not vary as much from job to job. They address the need to get things done through people. Interpersonal competencies tend to specialize with certain jobs such as sales, management coaching and customer service. At the most basic level, it is important for a job to be able to communicate effectively with other jobs. At an advanced level, interpersonal skills become effective persuasion or the ability to manage difficult customers on a regular basis. Remember, a competency must be measurable to be useful.

Here are some typical Interpersonal competencies:

- ◆ Management Coaching
- ◆ Customer Service Roles
- ◆ Sales Positions
- ◆ Interactive Teams

Your Action Statements within the Interpersonal Cluster should address the need for getting things done through people.

Interpersonal competencies typically include:
- ♦ Ability to persuade people to purchase a product or service
- ♦ Ability to persuade people to accept your ideas
- ♦ Coaching other people to get better
- ♦ Working closely with other team members
- ♦ Conducting meetings
- ♦ Making presentations to groups
- ♦ Resolving customer problems
- ♦ Writing documents

ATTITUDES, INTERESTS AND MOTIVATIONS

These are not really "competencies" because they have nothing to do with ability. However, they have everything to do with a person's willingness to perform the job. For starters, this cluster will always contain "wanting" or "not wanting" to perform the competencies contained in the other areas. But, it will also contain things you learned from the job analysis such as liking to travel, being away from home, frequent job changes, quality focus, shift work, etc.

Action Statements within the Attitudes, Interests and Motivation Cluster should address the likes, dislikes, attitudes, and preferences associated with the job.

Attitudes, Interests and Motivations typically include:
- ♦ Enjoys doing ..... <insert competencies here>
- ♦ Likes shift work
- ♦ Likes traveling
- ♦ Likes changes
- ♦ Focuses on quality
- ♦ Shows tenacity

PHYSICAL CLUSTER

You need to be careful here. Physical competencies are covered by the *American's With Disabilities Act* and are described under the *"Reasonable Accommodation"* section. The details of the ADA are far more involved than we can cover in this brief course; however, this section is where you include the special physical needs associated with performing the job. You will need someone who specializes in physical testing to test applicants for this area.

Some examples of Physical competencies include:
- ♦ Hearing
- ♦ Sight
- ♦ Physical agility
- ♦ Strength
- ♦ Speed
- ♦ Reaction time
- ♦ Endurance
- ♦ Verbal skills

ASSIGNING ACTION STATEMENTS TO COMPETENCIES

Take some time to assign your Action Statements to specific competencies. When you are done, take a 30 minute break. When you return, reexamine your list. Eliminate duplicates and consolidate statements where it makes sense. Try not to be too job-specific. Specific job details are between each manager and jobholder. Ask yourself if each Action Statement is clear, if it generally describes how the job is done and if there are enough Action Statements to describe the job successfully.

A note about competencies: the competency list you develop will never completely satisfy managers or individual jobholders because these people want detail, detail, detail! Selection competencies need to be general. Generality allows you the freedom to measure people with varied job experience fairly and accurately.

Managers and jobholders are free to take your competency list and tailor it to each position, but this kind of detail is only helpful to managers and individual jobholders.

If you have a competency with fewer than three items, consider combining Action Statements with another competency. **Remember to keep it simple.** Fewer is better. You don't want all the details; just the critical activities and competencies.

FINAL COMPETENCY LIST

A simple job may have only 5 to 7 competencies, while a professional or management job might have 12 to 14. Although some organizations will say they have lists of hundreds of competencies, these are either just different combinations of the basic competencies (i.e., problem solving = analysis plus judgment), or are very job specific (e.g., marketing analysis, financial analysis, sales analysis, etc.)

All interviews have limitations. It gets very difficult to measure more than 10 competencies without hearing applicants repeat themselves. If you insist on using a large number of competencies, you should consider supplementing interview data with simulations, exercises, cases, work samples, etc.

Be sure to get something within each Cluster. With a little luck, your final competency list might look something like this (oversimplified) example:

- ♦ Identifies and solves job-related problems
- ♦ Knows when to adjust the machine to balance speed vs. quality
- ♦ Chooses when to use the right maintenance schedule
- ♦ Possesses the ability to learn new information
- ♦ Learns to operate new equipment
- ♦ Frequently implements new safety procedures to minimize accidents
- ♦ Coaches other people to get better
- ♦ Instructs new team members to help them learn the job
- ♦ Works closely with other team members
- ♦ Supports co-workers when they are absent
- ♦ Volunteers for extra work when a team member is overworked
- ♦ Is willing to work long hours without complaint
- ♦ Enjoys a fast pace and changing work environment
- ♦ Is constantly concerned with making a quality product

(See Appendix B for reproducible worksheets)

SUMMARY

The job analysis is an important step in our behavioral interview system. Job analysis is entirely focused on the job and is independent of the people who fill the position. A well developed competency list will:

- ♦ Establish the business need and job requirements
- ♦ Guide the behavioral interview process
- ♦ Provide a measurable list of relevant competencies
- ♦ Clarify the job for both manager and jobholder
- ♦ Assure that you do not miss any important areas

Once you have a list of required job competencies, it is up to the jobholder to deliver on the required competencies. A job analysis provides legal documentation, business need and job requirements. Jobs with similar functions can be combined into one job analysis. The job analysis should include people who are thoroughly familiar with the job and who represent a demographic cross section of race, age, and gender. This group includes jobholders, managers and senior managers.

Once job data has been collected, it is converted into Action Statements that are progressively reduced to competencies. As a general rule, competency areas tend to remain constant across most jobs, but Action Statements tend to change with the position. Action Statements are the links between each specific job and its respective competencies. Attitudes, Interests and Motivations are not really competencies and are difficult to measure using common interview techniques. The job analysis process should be thoroughly documented. Job analysis need only be done once every few years or when the job changes significantly.

TEST YOUR HIRING KNOW HOW

1) What kind of information should you collect from your job content experts?

   a)   whether over or under 40

   b)   time with the organization

   c)   preferred kind of food

   d)   ethnic background

   e)   gender

   f)   time in the job

   g)   what makes a "good" producer "good"

   h)   opinions about what jobholders should be doing

   i)   how they feel about individual jobholders

   j)   their names

   k)   explicit job behaviors

2) From which job expert (Jobholders, Managers, or Senior Managers) do you acquire the following:

   a)   general comments on performance

   b)   how the job will change in the future

   c)   detailed questions

   d)   demographic mix

3) Place a mark beside each good Action Statement

   a)   close sales and get new business

   b)   persuade team members to change procedures

   c)   work closely with customer service

   d)   have a good attitude

   e)   learn new procedures to improve performance

   f)   work long hours

   g)   get along well with people

   h)   ask questions to clarify what was said

   i)   be concerned with quality

4) Match the following Competencies with a related Action Statement.

Competencies

1. Selling people a product or service

2. Persuading people to accept your ideas

3. Coaching other people to get better

4. Working closely with other team members

5. Conducting meetings

6. Making presentations to groups

7. Interacting with customers

8. Technical knowledge

9. Being able to identify and solve job-related problems

10. Ability to learn new information

11. Making good, on-time decisions

12. Keeping track of tasks and activities

13. Enjoy doing (competencies from Problem Solving, Planning and Interpersonal Groups)

14. Like/dislike shift work

15. Like/dislike traveling

16. Like/dislike changes

17. Focus/not focus on quality

Action Statements

a) make on the spot decisions balancing quality against production speed

b) trade shifts with other team members when asked

c) make four calls per day to prospective clients

d) know and be able to use four programming languages

e) teach co-workers to operate new equipment

f) manage and schedule projects so they finish on time

g) enjoy working on weekends and holidays

h) present technical ideas to nontechnical audiences

i) convincing other departments to change their paperwork flow so that your department will be more efficient

j) like the challenge of solving complex problems

k) be dissatisfied with anything less than perfect product

l) enjoy frequent changes and shifts in direction

m) lead the weekly management meeting

n) answer the phone and resolve customer complaints

o) read technical magazines to stay abreast of changing trends and technology

p) be able to do root cause analysis and recommend optimal solutions

q) travel 50% of the time

LESSON IV

Preparing for the Interview

OBJECTIVE OF THE INTERVIEW

In the previous chapters, you learned how behavioral interviewing is part of a system that is:

- ◆ At least ten times more accurate than traditional interviewing
- ◆ Content valid and legally credible
- ◆ Based on competencies determined from a job analysis

As we mentioned before, behavioral interviewing is a system with many parts. You should now have the first part in hand: a clear-cut competency list that you developed using information from your job experts. Now it is time to turn our attention to the applicant.

Whether it is called "event" interviewing, "targeted" interviewing, or some other term, all behavioral interviewing tools are intended to gather past examples of job behavior. If the applicant can provide reasonable evidence of past competency, then it is also reasonable to assume they can apply that competency in the future.

Note: behavioral interviewing is not the same as "situational interviewing." Behavioral interviewing looks "backward" by asking the applicant to describe what he or she has done in a specific situation. Situational interviewing looks "forward" by asking the applicant to describe what he or she would do in a specific situation. The weakness in situational interviewing is that it only measures if the applicant knows the "right" answer, not whether the applicant has used or actually can use the competency.

BACKGROUND, BEHAVIOR, CONSEQUENCE

A basic behavioral interview involves a series of linked questions, designed to draw information from an applicant's job experience. This information is then used to assess competencies required for the job at hand.

The questions are linked within a specific format to elicit the *Background, Behavior, and Consequence* of the event. We'll call this structure "BBC" for, you guessed it, Background, Behavior, and Consequence.

- ◆ **Background:** "Tell me about a time when you were faced with a difficult problem at Acme Inc." (Interviewer tries to learn about the situation faced by the applicant.)
- ◆ **Behavior:** "What did you do or say in response?" (Interviewer tries to learn what the applicant did or said in that situation.)
- ◆ **Consequence:** "What was the result?" (Interviewer tries to learn whether the applicant did or said the right thing.)

By using the BBC format for each competency, the interviewer maintains control of the questioning, is prepared to record answers, and is better able to follow the same structure for every applicant, every time.

WHAT WAS THAT AGAIN?

Your job as an interviewer is to gather accurate and complete data about situations in the applicant's background that are similar to those that will arise in your company's job. The questions should be general enough so that the applicants can relate to them. Here's an example of a bad interview question: "Have you ever fixed a model XT-173 before?"

Answer: "No."

That doesn't exactly open up the floodgates of conversation.

But the questions must also be specific enough so that the behavior is similar to one that the successful applicant might use on the job. Here's an example of a good behavioral interview question: "Tell me about a time when you faced a situation where you were given an unreasonable deadline? What was the situation? What did you do? What was the result?"

Answer: "Well, one time I ..."

This answer allows you to follow up with questions about the applicant's behavior and the resulting consequence.

The purpose of the BBC format is to encourage the applicant to provide a complete and thorough answer. If you don't get a complete or accurate example, you don't have good data. And poor data means placement missteps!

Questions are only successful if they elicit information on similar situations in the applicant's past, the reactions to those situations, and what the results of those actions were. Get answers to these questions, and you will be able to determine how the applicant will react to similar situations in the future.

"EMPTY" EXAMPLES

Suppose you asked the applicant one of your questions and got the following response:

> "We had a problem with the workflow, so I looked at what was going wrong and made a suggestion to my supervisor. In a few days it was fixed."

Sounds good, doesn't it? Too bad. The response is meaningless. There is no clear background, behavior or consequence. You need more information such as:

- ♦ Exactly what kind of problem did they have?
- ♦ Why was it a problem?
- ♦ What did the applicant actually do?
- ♦ Did the applicant's suggestion have anything to do with the solution?
- ♦ How did the applicant know the problem was solved?
- ♦ Is the problem similar to what the new job would require?

A BETTER WAY TO GO

Let's try again:

> "Our workflow process was confused because the record-keeping system was out of date. We were always working on the wrong projects at the wrong time and customers were getting upset. I suggested that we come up with a plan for keeping better records and made a suggestion to my supervisor. In a few days it was fixed."

Okay now? Well, you got much more of the background, but not enough of the behavior or consequence. Ask yourself what the applicant did? Just tell the supervisor? Not good enough.

Try this:

> "Our workflow process was confused because the record-keeping system was out of date. We were always working on the wrong projects at the wrong time and customers were getting upset. I analyzed the delay between the receipt of the goods and when the records were updated, developed a new tracking system on the computer that would eliminate the delay time, and made a suggestion to my supervisor. In a few days it was fixed."

How about now? Better, but the consequence is still unclear.

ONE MORE TIME

Try this:

> "Our workflow process was confused because the record keeping system was out of date. We were always working on the wrong projects at the wrong time and customers were getting upset. I analyzed the delay between the receipt of the goods and when the records were updated, developed a new tracking system on the computer that would eliminate the delay time, and made a suggestion to my supervisor. I was given approval to implement my suggestion. The out of date record keeping system was brought completely current within 30 days and our customer satisfaction rating improved by 50%."

Now we have a complete example.

You now know that the applicant was able to recognize a significant problem. You know the process used by the applicant to analyze the situation and solve the problem. And, you know the applicant's solution was effective.

This is useful data because we have insight into how this applicant solves problems and implements solutions. That information can be used to predict how the applicant would probably perform in the new job.

JUST THE FACTS

A common interviewer mistake is to use questions that will elicit different competencies with different applicants. For example, the question, "What would you say are your greatest strengths and weaknesses?" will get wildly different answers that cannot be compared to job requirements. Furthermore, it elicits responses that are extremely difficult to evaluate. For example, "I think I work too hard....and I should probably lose some weight."

Okay, what does an interviewer do with that kind of information?

Since your job analysis uncovered details about what the job needs, you need to prepare some questions that are focused on these competencies. Fortunately this is pretty straightforward. Let's dig into the Problem Solving Cluster and pluck out a competency or two.

As you recall, the following competencies are commonly found there:
- ♦ Having a certain type of technical knowledge
- ♦ Knowing how to use technical tools, etc.
- ♦ Being able to thoroughly analyze job-related problems
- ♦ Being able to make well-considered decisions
- ♦ Ability to learn and apply new information
- ♦ Making good, on-time decisions
- ♦ Developing strategies to accomplish a goal

DISCOVERING PROBLEM SOLVING COMPETENCIES

We'll pick the last two competencies: making good, on-time decisions and keeping track of tasks and activities. Using the BBC process, we get:
- ♦ **Background:** Give me an example in your job at Acme when you had to make a quick decision.
- ♦ **Behavior:** What did you do?
- ♦ **Consequence:** What was the result? (This question tests for problem solving and decision-making skills.)

Or:
- ♦ **Background:** Can you think of an example in your job at Acme when you had to reconcile conflicting tasks during your day?
- ♦ **Behavior:** What did you do?
- ♦ **Consequence:** What was the result? (This question tests for tracking and organizing skills.)

As a rule of thumb, you need two to three questions for every competency.

JOB ANALYSIS AS A SOURCE OF BBC QUESTIONS

Let's suppose our job analysis showed that the job required the following competencies:
- ♦ Being able to identify and solve job-related problems
- ♦ Ability to learn new information
- ♦ Coaching other people to get better
- ♦ Working closely with other team members to level the work load
- ♦ Being willing to work long hours without complaint
- ♦ Enjoying a fast-paced and changing work environment
- ♦ Being constantly concerned with making a high-quality product

Take some paper and write down three competency questions for each competency that you might probe in an interview. Use the worksheets in Appendix B.

SAMPLE COMPETENCY QUESTIONS

Did you get questions like this?
- ♦ Tell me about a time when you had to figure out a difficult problem on the job.
- ♦ Give me an example about when you had to learn new information about your job.
- ♦ Think back to a time when you had to coach a fellow team member to learn a new task.
- ♦ Tell me about when you had to work very closely with other team members.
- ♦ How often did you have to work long hours at Acme?
- ♦ Please describe the pace and rate of change at Acme.
- ♦ What kind of quality programs were you involved with at Acme?

It is not always easy to come up with good questions without "giving away" the answers, especially with Attitudes, Interests and Motivations. Measuring the Attitudes, Interests and Motivations is the weakest area of any type of interview - and a good reason why you should consider adding more measurement tools to your hiring kit. If you recall, additional tools include pencil and paper tests, exercises, case studies, role-plays, and motivational tests - all validated, of course.

EXPERT ANSWERS

Armed with your list of BBC questions, it is time to revisit your experts. (I assure you, if you do not revisit them at this stage you will end up arguing with them after the applicant leaves the building.) Expect the meeting with the experts to go something like this:

You: "Thank you for coming to this meeting. I have completed the job analysis on the Machine Operator position. As you see, I've taken your data, organized it into competency groups, and classified the job behaviors into competencies within each group. I've also prepared a list of questions that I plan to use to discover applicant competencies. Our task today will be to get your help clarifying answers I should listen for."

Them: "Huh?"

Research shows that only about 3 out of 10 managers are qualified to manage. The rest just squeak by. If you recognize that as many as 70% of your "experts" will have no idea what you are talking about, you will save yourself needless frustration. Just plow ahead. They will eventually tell you what you want to know. (You can, of course, increase your success rate exponentially by getting rid of the jargon when you speak to them.)

PATIENCE, PATIENCE, PATIENCE

Patiently go through each question, explaining that most of the applicants will not have the exact job experience desired, so you need to know what an acceptable response sounds like.

For example, your Competency question might be: "Tell me about a time when you had to figure out a problem on the job."

Possible responses might be:
- ♦ I examined the broken part, or
- ♦ I examined the entire machine to determine how the part broke, or
- ♦ I considered the impact of yesterday's raw material shipment and the effect of the humid weather on the machine's flywheel. Using this data, I analyzed...yada... yada...yada...

It is obvious which is the best answer, but which is the best answer for this position? Do you want a mechanical engineer to be your machine operator? While you might use the same question to hire a manager, blue-collar worker or engineer, the answers you should expect will change dramatically depending on what the job requires.

This information can only come from job experts. When you go over the questions with them, you need to find out what level of answer would be acceptable for that particular job. If you are hiring a cashier, a nice simple answer may suffice. If you are hiring an engineer, the answer ..would be significantly more complex.

WEIGHING IN ON COMPETENCIES

The last task of your job experts is to assign an importance weight to each competency. Not all competencies contribute equally to job success. For example, verbal communication might be very important, but analysis might be absolutely critical to success. Giving each competency a weight helps everyone in the interview chain focus on the most critical elements of the job. Ask your experts to privately distribute 100 points among the competencies, giving more points to the most important competencies and fewer points to less important competencies.

When each person is done assigning points, post all responses on a flip chart and get the group to arrive at an agreement.

Refer to the competency list you assembled earlier and distribute weights to each competency.

(Use the reproducible Weighing Competencies Worksheet in Appendix D.)

A FINAL NOTE ABOUT COMPETENCIES

Problem Solving competencies have the greatest range of responses because they encompass the greatest difference in job requirements. Consider, for example, the difference in Problem Solving competencies as a person moves from a janitorial position, to a machine operator, maintenance mechanic, operations engineer, design engineer, and a R&D engineer. As you go up in Problem Solving or Planning competencies, you will need people with equal or better Problem Solving or Planning competencies to ask the questions and evaluate the answers. We call these people "expert interviewers."

Interpersonal competencies have fewer levels. The specialties you need to investigate are selling skills, persuasiveness, customer service skills, team member skills, management coaching skills, and formal presentation skills.

Some competencies like "general communication skills" and "personal impact" are obvious to everybody. They are called "observable" competencies. You don't have to interview someone to tell if they can speak clearly and understand questions or not - it is perfectly clear when you hold a conversation. As to personal impact, you either see it or you don't. If you have to ask questions about a person's personal impact, you can be pretty sure they don't have it.

SUMMARY

Behavioral interviewing is considerably more accurate than traditional interviewing because it is based on a system of competencies, data gathering techniques and evaluation. The actual interview format depends on the interviewer's ability to collect from the applicant complete examples of background, behavior, and consequences (the BBC technique). The examples are converted into competencies and compared with job requirements. If the applicant cannot recall complete examples or the examples have missing parts, the data cannot be trusted. Information collected both from the job analysis and from job experts can be used to help an interviewer evaluate an applicant's responses. Giving weights to each competency helps the interviewer focus on the most important areas of the job.

TEST YOUR HIRING KNOW HOW

An inexperienced interviewer collected the following information from an applicant. Your job is to examine each example, and determine if it is complete or if it needs more data:

1) I worked very hard to put together a plan that would work.

      a) Needs more background data

      b) Needs more behavior data

      c) Needs more consequence data

      d) Complete example

2) My boss and I called on a customer who was having problems with delivery. I suggested we analyze the customers past orders to see if there was something we could do to anticipate their needs earlier. We fixed the problem and the customer was happy.

      a) Needs more background data

      b) Needs more behavior data

      c) Needs more consequence data

      d) Complete example

3) We had a terrible time keeping warm in the operations office so I bought a heater to keep us warm.

      a) Needs more background data

      b) Needs more behavior data

      c) Needs more consequence data

      d) Complete example

4) Well, the consultants tried to clarify the customer's needs after the sales people made promises they could not keep, but we always ended up arguing about the bills from project overruns.

      a) Needs more background data

      b) Needs more behavior data

      c) Needs more consequence data

      d) Complete example

5) We worked pretty much as a team, so whenever one of the staff was in over her head, we all pitched in to help get the work done.

    a) Needs more background data

    b) Needs more behavior data

    c) Needs more consequence data

    d) Complete example

6) I analyzed our problem and presented an idea for improving the efficiency in our department. The solution was very effective and reduced waste 15% in the first month.

    a) Needs more background data

    b) Needs more behavior data

    c) Needs more consequence data

    d) Complete example

7) One of our engineers was always late with project plans. This made the whole department look bad to the management team. A group of people and I took the engineer to lunch and explained our position and how delays in the project plans affected the entire department. He promised to do better in the future.

    a) Needs more background data

    b) Needs more behavior data

    c) Needs more consequence data

    d) Complete example

8) I spent every evening studying my manuals until I knew them by heart. Each day I would try something I learned the night before. Once, I learned that using an ABC prioritizing system would always get the most important things done. My supervisor saw me prioritize my work and told me that she had never seen someone clear a paper jam as quickly as I could.

    a) Needs more background data

    b) Needs more behavior data

    c) Needs more consequence data

    d) Complete example

9) My team worked all night to solve a problem that had been stalling production for months. Eventually we worked out a solution and put it in place the following week. The idea worked so well we were all rewarded with an extra day off.

    a) Needs more background data

    b) Needs more behavior data

    c) Needs more consequence data

    d) Complete example

10) My manager was having an argument with her boss about scheduling. I would have given the manager more time to work out her problems by herself, but her manager just told her to go home and cool off.

    a) Needs more background data

    b) Needs more behavior data

    c) Needs more consequence data

    d) Complete example

LESSON V

Measuring Applicant Competencies

BACKGROUND QUESTIONS

Getting information about the background that stimulated a certain behavior is an important beginning: it gives the interviewer an opportunity to assess the similarity of the applicant's situation with the job for which they are being interviewed. Some applicants have trouble thinking about situations they have faced in the past. Others have never worked in a company. In this case, the interviewer's job is to either give the applicant time to think of a response, or to suggest similar situations at home or at school.

Remember that not having data is just as bad as having poor data. An applicant who does not provide situational information is asking you to take a huge leap of faith that the right skills are there.

Since it is unlikely that an applicant has absolutely no life history, it is up to you to probe again, and again until some data surfaces.

A background interview probe might start out something like this:

> *Interviewer:* "So, Les, tell me about a time when you were faced with a difficult problem at work."

BEHAVIOR PROBES

The example that Les provided is weak. The interviewer must determine whether this is the kind of situation that Les might face on the job and find out why Les thought it was important. In other words, was this an elementary problem that could be solved by anyone, or did Les really use his problem-solving competency? Here is how the interviewer might probe further:

> *Interviewer:* "Why was that a problem, Les?"

> *Les:* "Our visitors were from overseas and it would have been a serious social offense if we had to feed them red meat. My assistant, who was supposed to order the special meal, was on vacation, and the lunch order was not placed before she left."

> *Interviewer:* "Go on."

> *Les:* "Well, I couldn't insult our guests, so I briefly excused myself from the meeting, asked another assistant to run over to the grocery store and had him place a special order with the manager."

Les described the background in more depth and moved on to behavior: where he described what he did in response to the situation.

VERIFYING CONSEQUENCES

It is very important to find out the final result of the decision and/or action. If the results turned out poorly, you need to determine whether it was the applicant's fault. Continuing with our example:

> *Interviewer:* "What was the result?"

> *Les:* "Things went from bad to worse. I didn't bring enough cash to pay for the food, so we missed having lunch altogether."

> *Interviewer:* "OK, Les. Give me another example..."

This was a negative consequence. But we are dealing with an experienced interviewer who will not make any judgment or adverse comments. She wants Les to keep talking and giving examples, so she will continue with her background, behavior and consequence questions. Eventually, she will get a pretty good idea about how Les solved problems in the past.

EVALUATING RESPONSES

Not all responses are quality responses. The next step in the behavioral interview process is to determine whether an applicant competency meets requirements of the job. You do this by giving each complete behavioral example a rating.

The best ratings are given to examples that are:
- complete and clear,
- recent,
- very similar to what is required in the new job,
- critical to the job,
- fully developed.

Remember that jobs change. The problem solving ability for one job may be significantly greater than for another. Before you can evaluate an applicant's answers you will need to know what the job requires. You should have learned this from the job analysis.

Each competency should have a rating. Rating techniques vary from organization to organization. We like to keep it simple.

Basically, all you care about is whether each competency is:
- more than needed in the job,
- just right for the job,
- not quite right (but might be coached),or
- unacceptable for the job.

Of course, there will be some highly weighted competencies that the applicant must have to do the job, but others will fall lower down the list of priorities. Just remember, your goal is to hire people who fit the requirements across the board. That's why you did the job analysis. Every time you compromise on an applicant's competency, you accept a job weakness that must be developed, trained, coached, or tolerated.

BEHAVIORAL EXAMPLES: APPLICANT WEIGHT

The interviewer started with a job analysis to define job requirements and business necessity. The data was converted into a weighted list of competencies and associated Action Statements. These formed the basis for a series of interview questions that assured thorough and complete coverage of the applicant's job-related skills. Next, the applicant was interviewed using a behavioral questioning technique that minimized error and misinformation. The last task was to determine if there is a match between the job requirements and Les' skills. This is done by verifying that the BBC examples are complete (incomplete examples mean incomplete data). Then the competencies and Action Statements from the job analysis are compared with the behavioral examples collected.

If Les' data is very similar to the kind of activities required for the job, the interviewer can feel confident in making an offer or recommendation to hire.

BEHAVIORAL EXAMPLES: EVALUATING THE APPLICANT

When you examine the overall results, you will find that an applicant tends to fall into a few general categories:
- **No Way!** Clearly does not have the right stuff for the job.
- **Mixed-Bag?** Possesses a mix of qualifications and weaknesses.
- **Just Right!** Meets every competency qualification.
- **Super!** Exceeds every competency.

It should come as no surprise that people who fall into the Just Right! and NoWay! categories have an obvious next step, but what about the other two groups?

BORDERLINE APPLICANTS

If you have a Mixed-Bag applicant, your job is more difficult. You can look at several things in this situation:

- ♦ Can I get more applicants into the selection funnel?
- ♦ Is the weakness in a critical area?
- ♦ Am I willing to invest time and energy in training and development?
- ♦ Can the job be changed to accommodate the weakness?

Super applicants tend to max out your competencies, so you have to look closer into their Attitudes, Interests and Motivations to see whether they will really like doing a job for which they are blatantly overqualified. Albert Einstein did not stay a patent clerk for long before he branched out on his own, so you should not expect Superman or Superwoman to be any different. When you have Super People you might want to ask yourself:

- ♦ Can the job be changed to match the strength?
- ♦ Do you have a more challenging position opening up soon?

SUMMARY

It is very easy to turn an interview into an interrogation, especially when trying to gather complete behavioral examples. Interviewers need to alternate between encouraging the applicant to give complete behavioral examples and keeping control of the interview.

Incomplete or false behavioral examples add error to the interview process. Converting behavioral examples to competencies links an applicant's past work experiences to job requirements. Assigning weights to competencies helps interviewers focus on the most important areas of the job. Assigning "fit" ratings to applicant responses helps interviewers evaluate the quality of the applicant's competencies.

The interviewer's goal is to find someone who is neither overqualified nor under qualified, but just right for the job.

Here is a list of the steps that you should take before, during, and after a behavioral interview:

- ♦ A job analysis provides task information about the job.
- ♦ Tasks are organized into competency clusters.
- ♦ Questions are developed based on each required competency.
- ♦ Questions are reviewed with job experts to get their input about desirable responses.
- ♦ The BBC technique is used to gather data about the applicant's past.
- ♦ Applicant's answers are organized into competencies.
- ♦ Applicant competencies are weighted against job requirements.

TEST YOUR HIRING KNOW HOW

1) Match the following

        a) job analysis

        b) weighting the competencies

        c) weak competency

        d) interview questions

        e) weighting the applicant's answers

        f) gathering "desirable" answers from the job experts

        1) defines what you are seeking

        2) gathers behavioral examples from the applicant

        3) helps evaluate responses

        4) helps define important areas

        5) helps the interviewer probe for examples

        6) may not be workable

2)   The following competencies were identified by job analysis

- Problem Solving (weight 10%)
- Learning (weight 10%)
- Persuasion (weight 15%)
- Technical knowledge (weight 20%)
- Written communication (weight 5%)
- Planning (weight 25%)
- Teamwork (weight 15%)

Four applicants were interviewed for the job. Their interview results are on the left. (M = more than required, J = Just right for the job, C= Not quite right but may be coachable, U = unacceptable) Classify them into the proper category: (1) No Way! (2) Mixed Bag (3) Just Right! (4) Super Person.

Applicant One
- Problem Solving (interview rating M)
- Learning (interview rating J)
- Persuasion (interview rating M)
- Technical knowledge (interview rating M)
- Written communication (interview rating J)
- Planning (interview rating M)
- Teamwork (interview rating M)

Applicant Two
- Problem Solving (interview rating J)
- Learning (interview rating M)
- Persuasion (interview rating J)
- Technical knowledge (interview rating J)
- Written communication (interview rating M)
- Planning (interview rating M)
- Teamwork (interview rating J)

Applicant Three
- ♦ Problem Solving (interview rating C)
- ♦ Learning (interview rating U)
- ♦ Persuasion (interview rating J)
- ♦ Technical knowledge (interview rating C)
- ♦ Written communication (interview rating U)
- ♦ Planning (interview rating C)
- ♦ Teamwork (interview rating M)

Applicant Four
- ♦ Problem Solving (interview rating J)
- ♦ Learning (interview rating C)
- ♦ Persuasion (interview rating J)
- ♦ Technical knowledge (interview rating J)
- ♦ Written communication (interview rating C)
- ♦ Planning (interview rating J)
- ♦ Teamwork (interview rating C)

LESSON VI

Errors and Omissions

NOT-SO-GOOD QUESTIONS

"When in doubt leave it out" is a good rule of thumb in behavioral interviews. For example, questions that have nothing to do with job requirements can easily be eliminated.

Some questions that could get you up close and personal with a lawyer include:
- "That's an interesting name. What nationality is that?"
- "Do you have someone to look after your children while you work?"
- "Do you have any handicaps that would interfere with the job?"
- "What religion are you?"
- "How old are you?"
- "When did you graduate from high school?"
- "Have you ever been arrested?"
- "Birthplace?"
- "Maiden name?"
- Asking for a photograph prior to hire.
- Questions about height or weight.
- Questions about marital status or children.
- Questions about mental or physical health unless determined to be "essential" under the Americans With Disabilities Act.
- "National origin?"

You really don't have to be a rocket scientist to recognize that these questions have nothing to do with the job. Forget them. They make your organization look unprofessional, and they don't have anything to do with the job.

OK QUESTIONS

Now that we have talked about the questions NOT to ask, here some questions that you CAN ask.
- Applicant's full name.
- "Have you ever worked for this company under a different name?"
- "Is any additional information relative to a different name necessary to check work record? If yes, explain."
- "How long have you been a resident of this state or city?"
- "Are you 18 years old or older?" (This question may be asked only for the purpose of determining whether applicants are of legal age for employment.)
- "Is your spouse employed by this employer?"*
- "Are you legally able to work in the United States?"
- Inquiry into the academic, vocational or professional education of an applicant and public and private schools attended.
- Inquiry into work experience.
- "Have you ever been convicted of a crime?"
- Names of applicant's relatives already employed by this company.*
- All questions about skills for performing the job.

* These questions may be asked if your organization has a written policy against nepotism.

ERRORS IN TECHNIQUE

In our example interview, Les was fairly organized and the interviewer fairly focused. This does not happen all the time. For example, some interviewers:

♦ Fail to control the interview
♦ Talk too much
♦ Allow the applicant to wander
♦ Do not probe for complete examples
♦ Do not encourage the applicant to talk
♦ Lead the applicant to the right answer
♦ Confuse being friendly with being friends
♦ Forget that their job is to gather data
♦ Treat applicants differently
♦ Turn the interview into an inquisition
♦ Try to remember what was said without taking notes
♦ Fail to prepare the applicant for the process
♦ Capture unclear examples
♦ Do not prepare by reviewing the data from the job analysis
♦ Do not complete every question with every applicant

These are all MAJOR mistakes!!!

FOLLOWING A PLAN

It is up to the interviewer to manage the interview process. This means knowing when to encourage conversation and when to take over. Keep in mind that the interviewer is testing for job skills.

When interviewers talk too much or try to get to know the applicant, they are interfering with the test. There is plenty of time before and after the interview to chat about the weather, but that goal should be secondary to gathering competency data. The interview is not a talk-show audition.

The same goes for note taking. Note taking is the most effective way to stay on track and stay focused on gathering data. When you take notes, you have some idea about when to probe for missing information and when to move on.

At the other extreme, behavioral interviews can turn into a pressure-packed interrogation session. This should also be avoided.

UNEQUAL TREATMENT

Anyone with a little interview experience knows how hard it is to remain objective. Sometimes you find yourself really liking an applicant and wanting to skip over questions. Other times, you find yourself disliking an applicant and wanting to stop the interview early. In either situation, you have added your own personal bias and error into the interview - and maybe set yourself up for a legal challenge.

Every applicant should be treated equally, without regard to your personal bias. The interviewer should always open the interview with a warm welcome and brief explanation of the process. The BBC process should be followed rigorously, and at the end applicants should be given a chance to ask any questions they might have.

ATTITUDES, INTERESTS AND MOTIVATIONS

Interviews are poor ways to measure Attitudes, Interests and Motivations because the questions tend to "beg" desirable answers. A rough rule of thumb when measuring Attitudes, Interests and Motivations is to trust negative data more than positive data. For example, if an applicant admits to hating human resources personnel, the answer can probably be trusted more than someone who claims to love them.

The best way to gain insight into the applicant's Attitudes, Interests and Motivations is to listen closely to "likes and dislikes" throughout the entire conversation.

TRAINABILITY

Some people seem to believe that anyone can be trained to do anything. They need to get out more. Training is a very good technique to improve or polish a skill that is already present, but training is a very expensive (and ineffective) way to fix a hiring mistake. Training may help some people manage time more effectively, but it will seldom develop a generally disorganized person into a master project planner.

For example, consider the challenge of training someone to be smarter, use better judgment, or learn more effectively. Training Attitudes, Interests and Motivations is even more difficult because they are often "non-negotiable" and often ingrained in the person's belief system. Anyone who says competencies can be trained has never trained competencies.

Each applicant comes to the interview endowed with certain traits and skills. If they fit the job, that's great. If they fall short and get hired in spite of this, get ready for a long and painful development period.

SHIFTING LEGAL STANDARDS

The judiciary seems to shift back and forth between giving and taking away "favored" status to certain groups, and there is little hope of this question being settled soon. For the interviewer, unless you are under a court ordered consent decree, your main obligation is to provide all applicants with a fair and equal opportunity to apply for any job for which they are qualified.

If you follow the job analysis, behavioral interviewing and evaluation process we outlined above, you should be able to do your job fairly. But always keep accurate records so that you can demonstrate that your hiring decisions were based entirely on job skills and behaviors.

GAMES PEOPLE PLAY

Behavioral interviewing is not a game where the interviewer knows all the answers and the applicant has to guess at the right ones. The interviewer's job is to determine whether there is a history of behavior that can be used to predict future behavior, not whether or not the applicant can remember applicable situations and behaviors during the interview.

It is okay to give applicants a list of competencies ahead of time and tell them to think about examples that will illustrate their skills in each area. This will save everyone a great deal of time and frustration.

LIAR, LIAR, PANTS ON FIRE!

Behavioral interviewing is effective because the interviewer knows what to look for and how to ask questions. The questioning technique is arduous and sometimes feels inflexible. But its high degree of accuracy depends largely on the fact that it is very hard to fabricate stories when the interviewer keeps probing for more and more details.

Terms often used to distract the interviewer along with some probing questions include:
- ♦ "We ...." But what did you do?
- ♦ "Should have ....." But what did you actually do?
- ♦ "And the problem was solved...." But what actually happened and how do you know it was successful?
- ♦ "Our team...." But what was your role?
- ♦ "Analyzed the problem...." But how did you do that?
- ♦ "We got together and worked it out." But what did you do?

STRETCHING THE LIMITS

Behavioral interviewing delivers solid results, but it has its limitations. Since it uses past examples to predict future performance, it presumes the applicant has actually had the experience. If there is no past experience, then there can be no predictions of future performance. This is especially true for people just graduating from school, reentering the workforce or moving from one job to another.

Using competencies helps translate past experiences into performance predictions, but the further removed the examples are from the target job, the greater the risk. This is one reason why promoting technicians to management jobs often has such disappointing results. A management job may contains the same competencies as the technician job, but will also require additional competencies associated with coaching and administration. Asking an applicant about his or her past competencies as a non-manager leaves a great deal of information undiscovered. When the technician is promoted, the weaknesses quickly appear.

There are only two ways to get data about new competencies and analytical skills. You must either put the applicant into some kind of training program or use management simulations such as cases and role-plays. This works for astronauts, commercial pilots and the military. Why not benefit from their experience?

SUMMARY

It is an easy "slide" from good questions to questions that could lead to a lawsuit for discrimination. A good rule of thumb is, "When in doubt, leave it out." All questions should be directly related to job requirements. Be sure to questions all applicants consistently, and gather complete and accurate examples.

Attitudes, Interests and Motivations are difficult to measure using interviews because the question tends to "beg" the answer. Interviewers should "listen between the words" or use a validated pencil and paper test to measure these items. Hiring an applicant who does not have all the right competencies usually will immediately lead to an expensive training need.

Many competencies are very difficult to develop or train. Giving an applicant a list of your questions before the interview will help them prepare better examples. Interviewers who fail to probe for good examples add an unnecessary margin of error to the selection process. Adding simulations and additional exercises to the interview can significantly increase the accuracy of hiring.

TEST YOUR HIRING KNOW HOW

1) Which of the following questions could lead to a lawsuit?

   a) Tell me more about where you came from.

   b) Who will watch your children while you are at work?

   c) Have you ever been arrested?

   d) Are you legally able to work in the US?

   e) Do you have any relatives who work in the organization?

   f) The job requires that you lift 50 pounds. Can you do this with reasonable accommodations?

   g) What church do you belong to?

   h) When did you graduate from high school?

   i) Tell me about a problem you solved in the past.

   j) Do you have any health problems we should know about?

   k) If you are hired, we will need to gather some data about your health. Is that acceptable?

2) Which of the following are effective interview techniques:
   a) Letting the applicant talk freely
   b) Giving the applicant a chance to ask questions throughout the interview
   c) Trying to be friends with the applicant
   d) Selling the applicant on working for your organization
   e) Probing to collect complete behavioral examples
   f) Cutting short an interview because the applicant is unpleasant
   g) Taking extensive notes
   h) Asking "what would you do if....?" Questions

3) Which of the following competencies are unlikely to change by attending a training program?
   a) analytical ability
   b) planning skills
   c) teamwork
   d) motivation
   e) attitudes toward work
   f) coaching skills

LESSON VII

Other Behavioral Interviewing Applications

EXPANDING BBC

Behavior interviewing is a proper test. It starts by knowing what you want to discover, then asking questions about past behavior, and using the answers to predict future behavior. Clearly, this is very useful for hiring the right people for the job, but how else can it be used?

For one thing, you can use it to diagnose training needs. First, you need to know what you want to measure. For example, you may determine that your sales clerks will also have some responsibility for inventory control. You can use the BBC interview format to probe and evaluate what skills your employees already have and how they might adapt to changing roles. A few questions later and you should have enough information to form a valid opinion of their skills and strengths, which is useful information for coaching and training programs.

Be cautious, though. In the last lesson we explained that behavioral interviewing has its limitations. These arise from not having the on-the-job experience required for a new position. Interviewing is a poor way to measure people for promotion to jobs that have more or different competencies. You may have read about this in the book, *The Peter Principle*.

The author explains how people are promoted until their career plateaus at their level of incompetence. As employees succeed, they are promoted until they are finally placed in over their heads, at which point the string of promotion ends and they are left in a position unsuited to them. It is not a good thing for an organization to be staffed with managers who plateau at levels of incompetency.

THIRD-PARTY INTERVIEWS

You don't always have to use behavioral techniques with the actual applicants. You can also use it to interview someone else about the applicant. For example, when you investigate the applicant's references, you can use the BBC to ask questions about situations, behaviors and consequences faced by the applicant.

This is a very efficient way to supplement and confirm data provided by the applicant, and it minimizes the amount of worthless cliche that typically comes from references.

SELECTION RATIOS

So now that you are a master of the behavioral interview, you should be prepared to "kiss a lot of frogs before you find your prince." An ancient scientific study has determined that you need to kiss about seven frogs to find a prince, on average.

Interestingly, the same is true with job applicants. Most interviewers find that somewhere between five and seven applicants are screened to find one applicant with the right qualifications. If your job requires more stringent standards, you might find the ratio to go as high as fifteen to one.

This is a strength, not a weakness of the system. It is the result of having a clear set of selection criteria and a very rigorous way to measure them.

PRACTICE MAKES PERFECT

Behavioral interviewing is a technique that takes more time to master than you might expect. Start by practicing on your friends or co-workers. Ask them for feedback and follow their suggestions. You might find it helpful to have someone observe your interviews as you learn. It is easy to overlook things in the interview, and they can point out areas you might want to work on. Once you've "worn out" your helpers, use a tape recorder and critique yourself.

As you practice more, you will gradually hone your technique and gather more accurate placement data. Practice, practice, practice.

FUTURE COMPETENCIES

As a general rule it is not a good practice to look too far ahead in either the job's or the applicant's future. It is a poor (and illegal) practice to evaluate someone for competencies required for a position they will not fill for years. The idea of selecting "young president" material is foolish and a waste of time. In fact, a 35 year study at AT&T indicated that people who became managers had a high drive for achievement, were good with people and were intelligent. No, really? The same could be said for a Saint Bernard! Not only is selecting people for positions that are more than two to five years in the future highly impractical, it could lead to a discrimination claim.

If you stay within a two- to five-year projection, your future leaders will surface naturally from among the competent people you hire using your behavioral interviewing system.

On the other hand, your organization might be transitioning to a new business culture. In this situation you might want to look for someone who meets a two-year vision. If you hire someone with competencies that don't match the job, you will probably gain an unhappy employee and more turnover than you'd prefer.

EXPLORATORY SURGERY VS. DIRECTED SURGERY

Exploratory surgery happens when surgeons don't really have an idea of what is wrong with a patient. They just open up the patient and hope that they stumble across what's wrong without causing too many additional problems. Directed surgery, on the other hand, happens when surgeons know exactly what the problem is and how to fix it.

Traditional interviews are like exploratory surgery. Interviewers don't necessarily have a sense of what to look for going into the interview. They just start the process blindly and hope that the right applicant will jump to the top of the pile. Behavioral interviews tend to operate more like directed surgery, since behavioral interviewers know exactly what they are looking for. When they see the applicant that they want, they make the hire.

PANEL INTERVIEWS VS. MULTIPLE INTERVIEWERS

Some people like the idea of panel interviews. I have mixed opinions. If panel members are each trained in behavioral interviewing and each one has a list of planned questions, they can be very efficient for the organization. But panel interviews tend to put a lot of pressure on the applicant, leading to "stage fright" and an inability to recall experiences. In fact, panel interviews might be a better measure of performance under stress than measurement of competencies.

I tend to prefer multiple interviews with different interviewers, each with a slightly different set of questions. This gives the applicant time to think about more examples and relate to different personalities. After all interviewers have gathered their interview data, they get together to compare notes. During the meeting, each person should present the competency, the BBC example and the rating. Other interviewers should probe or evaluate the accuracy of each response until they come to agreement. When all competencies are evaluated, the interviewers should come to general agreement about the applicant.

Multiple interviewers increase the accuracy of behavioral interviewing.

KEEPING DOCUMENTATION

The law is typically unclear about how much data you should store and for how long. I suggest that you ask your corporate attorney for an opinion. In general, clients tend to keep the summary data from the interview, the job analysis, and the list of questions on file. The actual time materials need to be kept varies with each client depending on local laws, the number of applicants and storage space.

SUPPLEMENTING BBC INFORMATION

There are many other measurement tools available to the hiring manager. Each one has its strengths and all should be validated before use.

- **The Case study:** A good way to measure mental ability because it has no clear course of action and inferences must be made from limited data, which can be mixed numerical and non-numerical data. This is very hard to score, but good for professional and management levels.

- **Planning exercise:** Measures the applicant's ability to sequence data, all of which is provided to solve the problem. This is very good for jobs requiring detailed planning and also good for professional and management levels.

- **Role-plays:** One-on-one controlled role-plays, situation-specific for sales people, managers, customer service, and team member jobs. This is the best way to measure interpersonal skills.

- **Intelligence test:** Measures general level of intelligence. They can be predictors of performance but carry a significant risk of adverse impact and require thorough validity documentation. These tests can easily be misused.

- **Personality test:** Measures different aspects of personality. These are very hard to validate, widely misused, and used primarily for clinical assessment. They are seldom used for actuarial measurement and usually are not job-related.

- **Motivational test:** Measure of likes and dislikes. They should be validated, since the results change with job and organization.

Scientific Selection keeps a comprehensive library of cases, exercises, motivational tests and simulations designed explicitly for accurate selection. They can provide up to 90% accuracy and are recommended for jobs that will have significant organizational impact such as sales, management, professional, etc. Using these tools requires confirmatory job analysis, validation and training.

SUMMARY

As we said in the beginning, just knowing how to ask questions is only part of the job. Behavioral interviewing is only one part of an effective selection process. The following steps will allow you to get the most out of a behavioral interview

- Conduct a job analysis to arrive at a list of measurable competencies.
- Prepare a list of competency-related questions.
- Review each question with other hiring managers and decide on desirable answers.
- Thoroughly cover each competency in the interview using the BBC approach.
- Convert the applicants' responses from your notes into competency categories.
- Evaluate the competency ratings against the required competency list.
- Discuss your data with other interviewers and arrive at a group consensus.

TEST YOUR HIRING KNOW HOW

Match the numbered term with a lettered term.

1. Best way to measure interpersonal skills
2. Diagnose training needs
3. Effective for interviewers but pressure-filled for applicants
4. Frequently misused
5. Good way to learn behavioral interviewing
6. Good way to measure professional and manager mental ability
7. Leads to higher turnover
8. Limit of behavioral interviewing
9. Measure of likes and dislikes
10. Measure sequencing activities
11. Reference checking
12. Set by organizational policy and local laws
13. Seven to one
14. Unfocused and error prone
15. Usually not job related and hard to validate

a. Another use for behavioral interviewing
b. Case study
c. Document retention
d. Hiring for skills needed in five-years
e. Intelligence tests
f. Motivational test
g. Observer feedback
h. Panel interviews
i. Describing on past examples
j. Personality tests
k. Planning exercise
l. Role-plays
m. Third party behavioral interviews
n. Traditional interviews
o. Typical number of interviews to hires

FINAL EXAM

1) Put the following activities in chronological order:

    a) Convert the applicants' responses from your notes into competency categories.

    b) Discuss your data with other interviewers and arrive at a group consensus.

    c) Do a job analysis to arrive at a list of measurable competencies.

    d) Evaluate the competency ratings against the required competency list.

    e) Prepare a list of competency-related questions.

    f) Review each question with other hiring managers and decide on desirable answers.

    g) Thoroughly cover each competency in the interview using the BBC approach.

2) What is the primary definition of behavioral interviewing?

    a) It is a series of good questions.

    b) It is a system of competencies, questions and desirable answers.

    c) It is another kind of interview technique.

3) Why does behavioral interviewing reduce turnover, increase productivity and reduce training time?

    a) Interviewers can get to know the applicant better.

    b) Applicant job skills are measured more accurately.

    c) The questions help gather more information about an applicant's personal interests.

4) Which of these people would make good job content experts?

    a) A 45 year-old male with 25 years job experience

    b) The only female with more than 12 months on the job

    c) A 23 year-old African American with 6 months experience

    d) The highest producers

    e) The lowest producers

    f) A good customer

    g) The manager of another department

    h) A 35 year-old male with 5 years experience

    i) A 40 year-old female with 7 years experience

5) Which of the following are tests?

    a) Pencil and paper exams

    b) Interviews

    c) Case studies

    d) Application blanks

    e) Role-plays

6) Why are traditional interviews no better than chance?

    a) They are based on job analysis.

    b) Interviewers can ask anything they like.

    c) There is usually no competency list to guide questions.

    d) Interviewers tend to ask illegal and leading questions.

7) Which document defines hiring practices?

    a) The EEOC act of 1997

    b) The Uniform Guidelines

    c) The Civil Rights Act of 1969

    d) The list of American Hiring Rights

8) When should you test your hiring practices using the 80% rule?

    a) Weekly

    b) Monthly

    c) Whenever you have time

    d) All the time

9) What is the primary purpose of a job analysis?

    a) To determine competencies

    b) To document job requirements and business necessity

    c) To serve as a guide to developing interview questions

    d) To help determine a set of uniform answers

    e) To support a legal defense, if challenged

10) Which of the following validation types most applies to behavioral interviewing?

    a) Construct

    b) Concrete

    c) Material

    d) Content

11) True or False: Employers can 'borrow' another organization's validation study and use it for their own jobs.

12) Which of the following statements is/are true about behavioral interviewing?

    a) It is a good way to select people for management positions who have never been managers.

    b) It uses past behavior to predict future behavior.

    c) It relies totally on a series of special questioning techniques.

    d) It is part of a comprehensive placement system.

13) What are the main competency groups?

    a) Problem Solving, Basic, Dairy

    b) Attitudes, Interests and Motivations

    c) Planning, Attitudes, Interests and Motivations, Single Parent

    d) Problem Solving, Planning, Interpersonal, Attitudes, Interests and Motivations

14) True or False: People are at complete liberty to redefine their jobs.

15) Which of the following is/are a measurable competency?

    a) Team player

    b) Problem solver

    c) Good natured

    d) Hard worker

    e) People person

16) Why should you gather demographic data during a job analysis?

    a) It's fun to get to learn private information.

    b) It shows you tried to be fair and equitable.

    c) To see if there are performance differences between different groups.

17) Who knows more about the details of the job?

    a) Managers

    b) Senior managers

    c) Jobholders

    d) Customers

18) What is the main purpose of an Action Statement?

    a) Puts behaviors into context

    b) Reduces error and improves clarity

c) Makes job analysis more complicated

d) Clarifies interview questions

19) Why are Attitudes, Interests, and Motivations hard to measure?

    a) Questions tend to "lead" applicant responses.

    b) Answers are often "socially desirable."

    c) They try to discover hidden competencies.

20) If you go over this number of competencies, you tend to get repeat answers:

    a) 7

    b) 12 to 14

    c) 10

    d) 15

21) Why should you revisit managers to review interview questions?

    a) They want to know what you are doing.

    b) They help define target answers.

    c) You want to demonstrate how much you know.

22) What is the primary purpose(s) of the BBC technique

    a) It reduces error.

    b) It helps keep the applicant from making up information.

    c) It helps the interviewer cover the complete job domain.

    d) It helps learn more about applicant competencies.

    e) It helps predict job success.

23) We had a production problem with the equipment. I analyzed the workflow and suggested that we change the feed rate. In a few days the problem was fixed. Needs more data about:

    a) Background

    b) Behavior

    c) Consequence

    d) Complete

24) Customers were complaining about the delays on shipping. I went to the shipping manager and explained our situation. I told her why we needed accurate shipping dates and what would happen to our customer base if the delays continued. She immediately hired two more shipping clerks. Needs more data about:

    a) Background

    b) Behavior

    c) Consequence

    d) Complete

25) Which of the following competencies varies most from job to job?

    a) Interpersonal

    b) Attitudes, Interests, Motivations

    c) Problem Solving

    d) None of the above

    e) All of the above

26) What are the four categories of applicants?

    a) No Way

    b) Too Tall

    c) Just Right

    d) Too Smart

    e) Super

    f) Mixed Bag

    g) Laundry Bag

APPENDIX A

Summary

There are three main steps to good selection:

Step One: Conduct a thorough job analysis to learn about the job. Different types of job analyses include:
- ◆ Interviews
- ◆ Critical incidents
- ◆ Visioning
- ◆ Surveys
- ◆ Confirming Questionnaires
- ◆ Rational discussions
- ◆ Statistical analysis

Step Two: Use the right tools to measure applicant skills. Every tool has its strengths and weaknesses. The following chart shows the respective accuracy percentage of each tool based on extensive research.

Percent Accuracy of Selection Tools*

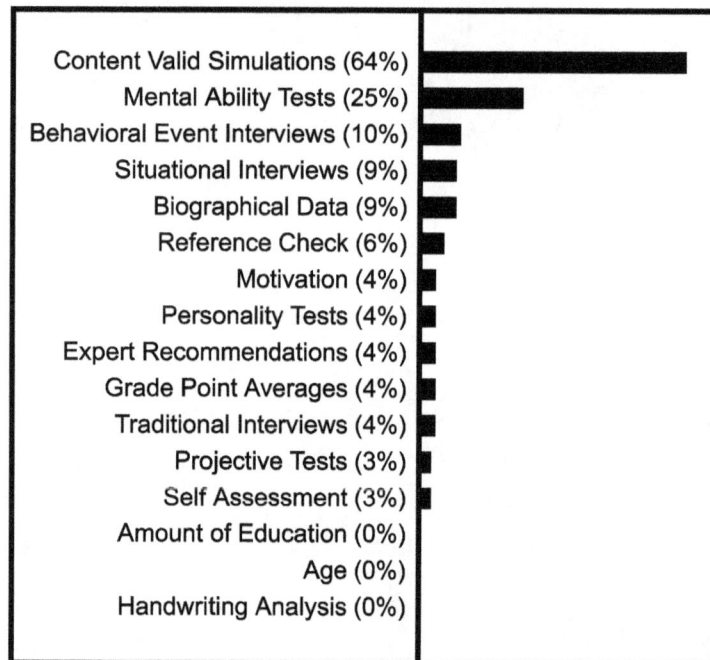

Content Valid Simulations (64%)	████████████████
Mental Ability Tests (25%)	██████
Behavioral Event Interviews (10%)	██
Situational Interviews (9%)	██
Biographical Data (9%)	██
Reference Check (6%)	█
Motivation (4%)	█
Personality Tests (4%)	█
Expert Recommendations (4%)	█
Grade Point Averages (4%)	█
Traditional Interviews (4%)	█
Projective Tests (3%)	█
Self Assessment (3%)	█
Amount of Education (0%)	
Age (0%)	
Handwriting Analysis (0%)	

*Adapted from a meta-analysis conducted by Hunter and Hunter, Psychological Bulletin, Vol. 96, 1984. Percentages have been rounded. "% Chance" refers to the unexplained variance.

Step Three: Be sure measurement scores reflect job requirements, based on:
- ◆ Content validation studies
- ◆ Criterion validation studies
- ◆ Effective cutoff scores

APPENDIX B

Competency Worksheets

Provided for all Competency areas. Reproduce as needed.

PROBLEM SOLVING COMPETENCY

Having a certain type of technical knowledge
Action Statements

1. _____
   _____

2. _____
   _____

3. _____
   _____

4. _____
   _____

5. _____
   _____

Knowing how to use technical tools, etc.
Action Statements

1. _____
   _____

2. _____
   _____

3. _____
   _____

4. _____
   _____

5. _____
   _____

PROBLEM SOLVING COMPETENCY

Being able to thoroughly analyze job-related problems

Action Statements

1. _____
   _____

2. _____
   _____

3. _____
   _____

4. _____
   _____

5. _____
   _____

Being able to make well-considered decisions

Action Statements

1. _____
   _____

2. _____
   _____

3. _____
   _____

4. _____
   _____

5. _____
   _____

PROBLEM SOLVING COMPETENCY

Ability to learn and apply new information
Action Statements

1. _____
   _____

2. _____
   _____

3. _____
   _____

4. _____
   _____

5. _____
   _____

Making good, on-time decisions
Action Statements

1. _____
   _____

2. _____
   _____

3. _____
   _____

4. _____
   _____

5. _____
   _____

PROBLEM SOLVING COMPETENCY

Developing strategies to accomplish a goal

Action Statements

1. _____
   _____

2. _____
   _____

3. _____
   _____

4. _____
   _____

5. _____
   _____

New Competency: _____

Action Statements

1. _____
   _____

2. _____
   _____

3. _____
   _____

4. _____
   _____

5. _____
   _____

PROBLEM SOLVING COMPETENCY

New Competency: ——————————————————————————————————

Action Statements

1. ——————————————————————————————————————

   ——————————————————————————————————————

2. ——————————————————————————————————————

   ——————————————————————————————————————

3. ——————————————————————————————————————

   ——————————————————————————————————————

4. ——————————————————————————————————————

   ——————————————————————————————————————

5. ——————————————————————————————————————

   ——————————————————————————————————————

New Competency: ——————————————————————————————————

Action Statements

1. ——————————————————————————————————————

   ——————————————————————————————————————

2. ——————————————————————————————————————

   ——————————————————————————————————————

3. ——————————————————————————————————————

   ——————————————————————————————————————

4. ——————————————————————————————————————

   ——————————————————————————————————————

5. ——————————————————————————————————————

   ——————————————————————————————————————

PLANNING COMPETENCY

Tracking tasks and activities

Action Statements

1. _____

   _____

2. _____

   _____

3. _____

   _____

4. _____

   _____

5. _____

   _____

Monitoring Processes or tasks

Action Statements

1. _____

   _____

2. _____

   _____

3. _____

   _____

4. _____

   _____

5. _____

   _____

PLANNING COMPETENCY

Planning project tasks
Action Statements

1. _____
   _____

2. _____
   _____

3. _____
   _____

4. _____
   _____

5. _____
   _____

Time Management tasks
Action Statements

1. _____
   _____

2. _____
   _____

3. _____
   _____

4. _____
   _____

5. _____
   _____

PLANNING COMPETENCY

Territory management tasks
Action Statements

1. _____

_____

2. _____

_____

3. _____

_____

4. _____

_____

5. _____

_____

Planning for contingencies
Action Statements

1. _____

_____

2. _____

_____

3. _____

_____

4. _____

_____

5. _____

_____

PLANNING COMPETENCY

Following up on assignments
Action Statements

1. _____
   _____

2. _____
   _____

3. _____
   _____

4. _____
   _____

5. _____
   _____

New Competency: _____
Action Statements

1. _____
   _____

2. _____
   _____

3. _____
   _____

4. _____
   _____

5. _____
   _____

INTERPERSONAL COMPETENCY

Persuading people to purchase a product or service
Action Statements

1. _____
   _____

2. _____
   _____

3. _____
   _____

4. _____
   _____

5. _____
   _____

Persuading people to accept ideas
Action Statements

1. _____
   _____

2. _____
   _____

3. _____
   _____

4. _____
   _____

5. _____
   _____

INTERPERSONAL COMPETENCY

Coaching others to improve

Action Statements

1. _____
   _____

2. _____
   _____

3. _____
   _____

4. _____
   _____

5. _____
   _____

Working closely with team members

Action Statements

1. _____
   _____

2. _____
   _____

3. _____
   _____

4. _____
   _____

5. _____
   _____

INTERPERSONAL COMPETENCY

Conducting Meetings

Action Statements

1. _____
   _____

2. _____
   _____

3. _____
   _____

4. _____
   _____

5. _____
   _____

Making presentations to groups

Action Statements

1. _____
   _____

2. _____
   _____

3. _____
   _____

4. _____
   _____

5. _____
   _____

INTERPERSONAL COMPETENCY

Resolving customer problems

Action Statements

1. _____

   _____

2. _____

   _____

3. _____

   _____

4. _____

   _____

5. _____

   _____

Writing documents

Action Statements

1. _____

   _____

2. _____

   _____

3. _____

   _____

4. _____

   _____

5. _____

   _____

ATTITUDES, INTERESTS, AND MOTIVATIONS

Attitudes

Action Statements

1. _____
   _____

2. _____
   _____

3. _____
   _____

4. _____
   _____

5. _____
   _____

Interests

Action Statements

1. _____
   _____

2. _____
   _____

3. _____
   _____

4. _____
   _____

5. _____
   _____

ATTITUDES, INTERESTS, AND MOTIVATIONS

Motivations

Action Statements

1. _____

   _____

2. _____

   _____

3. _____

   _____

4. _____

   _____

5. _____

   _____

PHYSICAL REQUIREMENTS

Hearing
Essential Elements

1. _____
_____

2. _____
_____

3. _____
_____

4. _____
_____

5. _____
_____

Sight
Essential Elements

1. _____
_____

2. _____
_____

3. _____
_____

4. _____
_____

5. _____
_____

PHYSICAL REQUIREMENTS

Physical Agility
Essential Elements

1. _____
   _____

2. _____
   _____

3. _____
   _____

4. _____
   _____

5. _____
   _____

Strength
Essential Elements

1. _____
   _____

2. _____
   _____

3. _____
   _____

4. _____
   _____

5. _____
   _____

PHYSICAL REQUIREMENTS

Speed
Essential Elements

1. _____

_____

2. _____

_____

3. _____

_____

4. _____

_____

5. _____

_____

Reaction time
Essential Elements

1. _____

_____

2. _____

_____

3. _____

_____

4. _____

_____

5. _____

_____

PHYSICAL REQUIREMENTS

Endurance
Essential Elements

1. _____
   _____

2. _____
   _____

3. _____
   _____

4. _____
   _____

5. _____
   _____

Verbal
Essential Elements

1. _____
   _____

2. _____
   _____

3. _____
   _____

4. _____
   _____

5. _____
   _____

APPENDIX C

Sample Question Worksheet

Reproduce as needed.

CLUSTER: _____

COMPETENCY: _____

Background Question
_____
_____
_____

Behavior Question
_____
_____
_____

Consequence Question
_____
_____
_____

APPENDIX D

Weighing Competencies Worksheet

Reproduce as needed.

Cluster	Cluster Weight	Competency	Competency Weight
Problem Solving			
Planning			
Interpersonal			
Atitudes, Interests, and Motivations			
Physical			

ANSWER KEY

INTRODUCTION

(1)b, (2)c, (3)c, (4)b, (5)d, (6)c, (7)d, (8)b, (9)a

LESSON I

1) c, a, d, b
2) c

(350 total applicants - 300 non-protected group members = 50 protected group members; 200 non-protected group hired /300 = 66% hiring rate; 66% x 80% rule = 53%; 53% x 50 protected group members = 27)

3) d
4) false
5) I = (b, c, e, f, i, j, k)   II= (a, d, g, h, l, m)
6) a=2, b=1, c=3

LESSON II

1) (I = a, g, j, m,) (II =d, e) (III =c, f, i, p) (IV=h, l, n,) (V=b, k, o, q)
2) False
3) b, c, g
4) b, f, g, i

LESSON III

1) a, b, d, e, f, g, j, k
2) (1, c, d) (2-a) (3-b)
3) b, e, h
4) (1- c) (2- i) (3-e) (4-b) (5-n) (6-h) (7- o) (8- d) (9-q) (10- p) (11- a) (12-f) (13- j) (14- g) (15-r) (16-m) (17-k)

LESSON IV

1) a, b, c
2) c
3) c
4) b
5) b, c
6) a, b
7) b, c
8) d
9) a, b
10) a, b, c

LESSON V

1) (1-a) (2-d) (3-e) (4- b) (5- f) (6-c)
2) Answer (No Way = c) (Mixed Bag = d) (Just Right = b) (Super = a)

LESSON VI

1) a, b c, g, h, j
2) e, g
3) a, c, d, e

LESSON VII

(1=l, 2=a, 3=h ,4=e, 5=g, 6=b, 7=d, 8=i, 9=f, 10=k, 11=m, 12=c, 13=o, 14=n, 15=j)

FINAL EXAM

1) a, b, c, d, e, f, g,
2) b
3) b
4) b, h, i
5) all
6) b, c, d
7) b
8) d
9) a, b, c, d, e
10) d
11) false
12) b, d
13) d
14) false
15) b
16) b
17) c
18) a, b
19) a, b
20) c
21) b
22) a ,b, c, d, e
23) a, b, c
24) c
25) c
26) a, c, e, f

SCIENTIFICSELECTION.COM

ScientificSelection.com is a no-nonsense, bottom-line focused consulting organization that specializes in:

♦ Implementing turnkey selection systems
♦ Developing customized tests and exercises
♦ Validating tests and exercises
♦ Auditing selection systems to ensure EEOC compliance and effectiveness
♦ Developing valid personality tests that identify high producers
♦ Assessing internal talent
♦ Conducting customized behavioral interviewing programs
♦ Studying jobs to determine competencies
♦ Integrating selection, training, and performance management systems

ScientificSelection.com, LLC
36 Emerson Hill Square
Marietta, GA 30060
770-792-6857

Our core competency is helping organizations make better hiring, promotion and placement decisions....

- One day in-house BBC Workshops for 6 to 8 people

- Installing turn-key hiring and promotion systems that accurately screen-in qualified applicants and screen-out the rest

- Developing and validating custom tests and exercises for hiring, benchmarking, career planning, or promotion that actually work

- Assessing employee bench strength for mergers and acquisitions- learn which employee skills can and cannot achieve the company business plan

- Reducing legal exposure arising from illegal or ineffective hiring and placement practices - audit HR hiring and promotion systems for legal compliance

- Reducing employee confusion by integrating hiring, performance appraisal and training competencies - ensure that employees are hired, managed, trained, and appraised on the same competencies

- Accurately predicting employee performance using artificial intelligence to reduce hiring and promotion mistakes.

Order 10 or more SuperSelection workbooks for $54.95/copy. Free FedEx delivery anywhere in the lower 48 states....

Please enclose a check, include the number of copies you would like to purchase and provide the following information:

Ship to: Name: _____
       Address: _____
       FedEx will not deliver to a PO box.
       City_____
       State, ZIP_____
       Contact Phone Number: _____